Daylight

Poems by Angela Karee

Copyright © 2019 by Angela Karee
All rights reserved.

For Jordan & Jakada
Grace & Mercy

&
In Memory of Mrs. Kandi Bryson Weathers
who taught me to love words

Contents

Contagion. 7
A Lesson of Histories, 9
Origin Story, 11
Origin Story (Revisited), 13
Game Day, 15
We Ask To Be Delivered, 17
Corps, 19
The Unnamed Wars, 21
The War Begins, 23
The End and The Beginning, 25
Niggadisniggadat, 27
Ferguson & Elsewhere, 29
Act of Resistance, 31
#, 33
Aubade, 35
Autopsy, 37
The Ghetto Lottery, 33
Tomorrow's Daily Caller Headline, 41
the king's english, 43
Thoughts & Prayers, 45
All the Silences, 47
us against us, 49

61st Street, 53
Garden Statues, 55
Learning the Count, 57
Brokedown Palace, 59
Come Down Town, 61
Collateral, 63
A Framework, 65
Urban Garden, 67
Whatever Wreckage Remains, 69
Englewood, Chicago, 71
I Want to Go Home, 73
Rarely Break Bread We, 75
In Just Summer, 77
Missed Connection, 79
Box the Girl, 81
Girl Gone, 83

CONTAGION

If these are the last words I ever write
Amen

I hope they balm

I hope they bruise

I hope they choose
wisely

If these are the last words I ever write
I want them

salt on your tongue

I want them
melt in your arms

Unadorned

The bullet & the teeth

I want these words lost
highway

highway

the capture & the hunt

If these are the last words I ever write
I'm sorry—

What I mean to say is--

I'm sorry—

I want my words to mean whatever
You think they mean
Whatever you say

What do you say—
Your mouth, like a heart
slit open—?

But if these are the last words I ever write

I hope they love you

& leave you broken

A LESSON OF HISTORIES

Think the laws of the physical world—
    A well-whooped dog and the space to brood

Think less
    as the only constant

Think shackle-chic and top-to-toe
    Oceanwares

Think whip-crack &
    rope-burn

Think the nightmare is over

Think bloodhound
    up-in-smoke
    fire hose justice

Think nightstick & noose

Think flight is the answer

Think red line &
    black ball
    pins designed to contain

Think Project

Think crack rock

Think gun run
    an iron for iron trade

Think false witness

Think probable cause

Think stop
    & frisk

Do not resist

Think this a theory
   or

History enough to break a man?

ORIGIN STORY

And in this desert, neglect makes rebel
of grass blades. Glass blades through,
like a fingernail through the eye.
What we do not see, we cannot say.
What we cannot say coagles in the throat,
collects in a pool of unsaid things
we tread wary over, like some bootleg Jesus.

But the liquor's spilt and so's the blood.
We keep cussing and praying for an end,
all of us alike in our hieroglyphed skin,
our thirst and desire.

We are everything
like the legends of our fathers
who were ghosts before they were ghosts, only
that is not the whole story...

So, when did we begin to believe and why
were we in need of such believing—
the stories told about our makeup,
about how the thing acts always against its own
best interest—
walking upright when it should cower
raging when it should lapse into song

praise for the fool-proofed god
who crafted—in his image—
such a monstrous thing as us
nose-spread & high hung,
spilling seed for another man's plow

ORIGIN STORY (REVISITED)

You are made up
of made up parts
Pick-n-Pulls
whatever god
found lying around
that didn't fit
to something else

Which is why
your knuckles shrill
& your knees
forecast the weather

You are not beautiful
by any measure
of beauty that matters

And your hide reeks
of the seasons too
and of too much sun

Even your bones grow
ugly underneath
that cavity of skin

your muscle
slithering off the bone
into its own
addled display
while your teeth & toes
clatter on

You will forever be

footnote
 to your own story—

the defect of your soul
having been bled from you

& collected here
where even the ground
won't open to take you in

GAME DAY

The earth seethes underneath
heaves itself into pits
into which the young among us
hurl each other for sport

The scattered few gardens of the city rejoice
There will be no drought this year
There will be no hunger season

The mothers will gather babies
in the apron of skirts, sink elbow deep
into prayer. Some will collapse
under shade of a tree and take a break
from grieving.

Someone should tell them
of the ground on which they settle—
that kingdoms have been built here
only to watch them fall.

We Ask to Be Delivered

We ask to be delivered

      from the evil that lords the streets

          Stand

             Amen

Brush the asphalt from our knees

            then ride the bullet—

      our mouths

      full of wind and flies too much

to talk about what a kind of dis-

      loyalty it is

           to see it & know & not

           call it out by name—

      our loves—

    the shadows   we bare

who   & for whom

    we fear

        all while claiming   *We*

            ride or die 'round here   hoping

      for the former, knowing

    all too well

how readily a body   grows wings

    'round here

    because we've seen this

      metamorphosis before:

   the brown skin

  stippled black, peeled back to reveal

the rage

   white tissue of muscle, gristle

    slithering the bones

     the quiet rivulet

   of piss and tears that whets these streets

  softens them

opens them up   to accept

  our shadows

    each a token

     a sacrifice

   an offering

  of surrender

Stand

  Amen

    Brush the asphalt from our knees,

      then ride the bullet

CORPS
> *"We are winning the war..."*
> -U.S President George W. Bush

Who ever wins and how
Much, so much is loss?
The vein of
earth slit open—bodies,
whole bodies slip through

THE UNNAMED WARS

No chameleon clothes smolder atop the piles of white tees and jeans
No patches, no gold medallions dazzle the sunlight to be trinketted
upon retrieval and flight home—

No—the mothers flock to scene in housecoats, headscarves,
determined to decipher flesh from flesh—a pointless task.
Everywhere, clean underwear, cotton socks, Vaselined skin.
Yet, even the teeth are mangled

Besides, the boys were lost long before this heat stroke—
Before the rains came and the wildfire sent to quench them,
When good air stayed the morning and only newborns owned the moon

The boys were lost long before that first day and naming and
circumcision, their fathers chased from call range,
their mothers' legs left bare, cycling the air

THE WAR BEGINS

The war begins, but they do not tell you
your mission or on which side of the cause you fall
So, you are all instinct
rising to the level of the next man's chest.

You are a split second and time infinitum

You do not see the line that draws you
Nearer to your enemy—a man, just like you
scared shitless, like you,
who spit in the same vein the same shit
that split open some bitch's legs, like you
who knows no better than you that he, too
was borne from the labyrinth
of another man's addled recess,
born without benefit
of his own understanding,
of that which came before him or ever since.

And, well, since you are the gods of this day,
I guess it is to you that I pray.

THE END AND THE BEGINNING
                              -after Wislawa Szymborska

After every war
someone has to clean up.
Things won't
straighten up themselves, after all.

Someone has to peel the bullet-
laden bodies from the pavement, pull off
the tattered clothes, stitch the holes
of jeans, scrub clean the knees.

Someone has to rattle
shopping carts through the streets,
collecting & redeeming
spent casings, beer cans, unbroken bottles.

Tomorrow's headlines
will get it twisted
count the dead among the living,
mispronounce the deeds.

No one will witness.
Someone will take a broom to glass.
Someone will take a glass to face.
Someone will take the meat home to eat.
No one will witness.

Someone else must know this:
must have, in the endlessness of wars,
memorized the list of things to do,
the tedious chore of order.

That someone has to snatch down
the red tape and board up doors,
face the sign to Open, stock Swishers,
make change.

We all will listen

from rolled up car windows, front porches,
couches in front of muted TV,
for when the fury ends

for the wound that silence make—
like rocks through windshields;
like bullets through bodies;
tires balding corners,
taking out street signs, small children.

NIGGADISNIGGADAT

A nigga like you
should be in somebody's
poem

A nigga rhymes
with bigger things
Triggers things
we don't like to face

But a poem is a beautiful place
for a nigga to hide
because words have power in them
and niggas is a force
to wreck with a word like *nigga*

nigga—crafter
of ancient words into new meaning—
a whole new language
struggled through because a nigga like you
needs to join the conversation
Say something poetic &
apocraphetic or whatever,
Just speak nigga!

Because silence is a language
of the dying

Ferguson & Elsewhere

Facts collapsed on the hot concrete, blistering under the sun
For hours as police dutifully gather their stories and the facts

The fact is the cop did his job or he'd be the one dead,
His mother on TV in tears, clamoring for the facts

The boy must've thought blunts make the body bulletproof
They don't, but how, now, might we wish this was fact.

We cannot let our emotions get the best of us in situations like this
We *must* look to the facts.

It is true you cannot measure the level of fear in another man's heart
A demon, he said, whose perception is defensible fact

The one witness closest to the action, whose story didn't change
Turned out to be accomplice to thief, so you can never trust his facts

The white shirt spoke in bold, black tones.
Death is matter-of-fact

Questions raging through the streets for weeks in symbolic surrender
Are assured that race was never a factor

Justice is a crapshoot and a thin blue line
It is not a checker of the facts

This is a thing Angela wrote to find beauty in a thing that isn't
This is a poem. It is hardly a fact.

ACT OF RESISTANCE

… dramatic footage shot from a different angle reveals

[the black body]

just as dead or dying

as in our initial views…

Police state that…

…they cannot validate

the authenticity of the footage

but…what is clear…

[the black body]

called / was cause for alarm

[the black body]

had / was a weapon

[the black body]

is in / defensible

against a bullet

a blue hail

a black haze

                                                    another body's
                                                    alleged fear

Still, in this hour

        questions remain…

Will

                      [the black body]

ever comply

                            with all orders to cease & desist or

~~will~~ must

                    [the black body]

                        persist?

\#

I am   mother

     of a feared thing   most

Dark scrawl

     of it(s) body

     like a pen inked dry

as I'm writing this.   *Why*

     my precious? Why *my* precious?

Such a natural thing—

     such like the natural

     winds and rains and flames

that rip the natural limbs from all   of God's

     manmade things

to make study of:

     These ones   heirlooms

of incriminating marks

     from birth turning under the sun

more black

     Blacker still

     'til they're ashen

'til they're lightless

        and by then

it don't matter

        Ask me after   if I'd have

spread my legs   far wider

than I ever had before

        and beared down at all

when the island-tinged woman

        in her festive wears warned

        Not yet honey, you'll tear

AUBADE

Last night was the last night, but who could have known?
Your normal's broken open—the bright yellow morning sprawling
to a noiseless, numbing gray that will only end when you do

Your baby spilled onto the sidewalk,
beneath the window from which you've called him—my God—
a million times home before the streetlights, the thunderstorms,
the shit brewing on the corner hits the fan

You, knowing of nothing else to do,
take the cold throne because it comes naturally,
but skip the breakfast meats and coffee
pull on some clothes, ghost down the stairs and out the front door

This day could have been the start of anything—
there are tires on the surface of the roads; shoes and the bodies
that fill them pressing on. There is everything in defiance
of the new reality: a world one boy short
A city, late in waking, cold and grimy as ever

Oh, to see you in the shadow of this soft sunlight,
prostrate on the ground, the whole of you coming undone,
trying your damnedest to siphon him back home

AUTOPSY

First we ask why
slide the blade down
the body's center & pry
open the door to where
all answers can be found

I have never been so afraid
to walk a corridor alone
but they tell me this is the one
that leads to the heart
So, I follow the history's trajectory
backward, finger first…

No matter how many times I do this,
it doesn't get any cleaner
or go any easier—

They don't want us
opening old wounds
or wounds that haven't healed
or wounds as yet inflicted

They want us sweat soaked,
Slab stable
Silent

But we continue

We have to know the damaged extent;

The clear cause

The immeasurable level of fear
that always kills us

THE GHETTO LOTTERY

Unlucky at birth
we try an amalgam
of extraordinary feats
to quick turn the fortune—
out the womb
straight shootin'
jumpshots by alleylight
craps in the gangway
anything running
for a come up

The going's slow
for those of us who ain't got
beats or handles or knows
somebody who do
so we spend our last
dollar for a quarter
drop that quarter on a dime
and be damned
tired of losing,
tired of watching
the fruits of our labor
labor to waste
in these streets

So we just give it to god
and pocket the gold—
This here bet, the sure shot
The odds, forever in our favor

Tomorrow's Daily Caller Headline:

Brave Officer Prevents Unemployed Thugs
From Robbing Public Resources

Defender of the Peace Tames Rowdy Negros:
No Damage Reported

A tree branch is the oldest lethal weapon
in the book

These children are obviously eco-terrorists—
an Earth First sleeper cell

They had broken tree branches—
were obviously working
on their Jr. Black Panther clubhouse

Shoulda been building a shoe shine stand
like the good colored folk did back in the day

How did those kids get away
from their rightful owners in the first place?

Back in those days, when a boy was caught
being black, he would 'fess up
and take his bullets like a man.

The cop was a pussy—
should have put at least 20 in that kid

Perpetrator of black-on-tree violence
Violent tree mutilator
Potential pine cone thrower

A drawn weapon,
a program to arm all trees
is the only way to protect the neighborhood,
to prevent future occurrences.

You know how terrifying 11 year olds can be, hell
kids in my neighborhood are fully operational
battlestars aiming their particle beams at the moon

THE KING'S ENGLISH

don't use like
like the hook of a song

when writing
don't use apostrophes
if nothing's missing

or possessed

know the difference

between rather & whether
between weather & whether
between here & there

do not use the double negative,
but the double entendre is always
apropos

do not appropriate our language
to fit your own jagged swagger—

in this Country, we
pronounce the hard *r*

The,
a slip the tongue between the teeth

To be understood
you must understand

every syllable matters

sometimes more than lives

Thoughts & Prayers

After the smoke,
the silence--
A darkness encased
in darkness
We cannot agree
who fired first
We cannot agree
it matters
It matters
But after the silence,
no stillness
And after the stillness,
no settle
We history all wrong,
then repeat

ALL THE SILENCES

All the silences in between
Our first blood struck and yours
Have drowned our sorrow

When we were mourn
When we were rage
When we were question mark burning
You shrugged

Now we must share the burden
Of this tragedy together

All *the whatever shall be dones*
The *what else can we dos*
Just let them eat each other
We'll snack on what is left

What is left
Is an arm locked circle and a shrine
Drummed up fears to drum up tears
For what was always solemn and shame
But now is made holy again

US AGAINST US

us against us
uprising   fire

which flies from the lips
the fingertips

you
bruise maroon

me blue black & smoke

me thick tongued
        resistance

you wolf-cry
you curse

you flag-cloak & brass
    pen-stroke
        ink heavy in the margins

me: ink
heavy in the margins

        you born
        me bred

in another time & place
            we are not altogether
        different

        you & me

        god conjure
        & crave

        the life breathed word into

a wishbone halved & planted

in steaming black earth or else
to high heaven   buried

      up to the neck in clouds

TWO

61st Street

milk jugs of kerosene and water
electricity borrowed
from the building next door—
a come up the back way
rises giving way
hammered, nailed, hammered again.
flies let in
the screened in back door
an open stove in winter
all of us
crammed into the tightest, brightest room—
a way made from anything
        but *words?* words could never
nigger rig a cable line
make a whole meal of sugar and rice
or roll up sleeves to scrub floors, plant mustards or even
bury, resurrect the dead

GARDEN STATUES

After church and we, still in our Sunday best,
go outside to play—warned
by our mothers not to get the good clothes dirty,
not to step off the stoop, off the block, out of sight.

Outside, free of a watchful eye, we find the wild in us,
leaping from one escape to the next—
our jungle, stone gray. Ferocious.

We are skinned by the teeth of the boys
who have already survived this.

Or haven't.

Theirs are not lessons we are old enough to learn,
so we lean in—jump, swing, sway, fall,
rip the knees of slacks that won't ever be patched

We get older. We go home again. Perch ourselves
on the front porches where we grew ourselves into men,
carrying with us our stories
and all of our scars.

Learning the Count

Six blocks
Seventeen houses of worship
A shrine of teddy bears and Mylar each
at the four-way stop
Eleven bottles
Eleven brown paper shrouds
A dozen or so chicken places
Nowhere to throw the bones
One bench
Two hard luck stories
Not a single bus in sight
Three little minutemen and
A jack-knifed fence
One hand closing into another
A hundred twenty-three soles
Scratching the surface of this morning
Twenty four corners
Eight different ways to grow wings

BROKEDOWN PALACE

House to the rafters
down to the studs
with no people inside

In the basement
all the natural light
Sneaks off
towards the dawn
but returns before
the sun goes down
when it would truly be missed

In the living room
the hardwood's faint
echo, a hallway
that leads to
but barely returns

and the kitchen only hopes
for fire

In the bath, with
so little space to wait &
no place for the waste's removal

Up the stairs
three large bedrooms for dreaming
A fourth for taking flight

COME DOWN TOWN

All the sainted people
of the quaint little
come down towns
fear news of apocalypse.
They shelter in place
peeling hands
with their teeth for feed,
Their eyes, wiled
a hair, like the heathens' domain
Many roads lead here
Many leave
grooved blue into the vein
and the children?
the children would ransom
their dream for wings

COLLATERAL

Each morning when I wake, I check my phone
to see how much the world has changed;
if, during the hours of my rest,
a whole village has been razed from theirs
and marched off the flat edge of the world
or whether they have been planted,
like the tattered little flags they are,
in the hinterland of a madman's dreams
Has someone used the cloak of night
to gank tomorrow's sun?
the days have been so hazy here.
Elsewhere, I do not know of clouds,
or landscape, or treachery of road
that defends against centuries old war;
But I do imagine a momentary peace
that breezes through the open windows
from which they pretend surrender,
pray for rescue, or smile and wave hello.

A Framework

presuppose home
outside the boundary
of heart, before heart
had a name, and name,
itself, a function

claim it shallow
claim it hallowed
claim it deep,
narrow path
bruised core—
halve it
live well

URBAN GARDEN

I want space safe enough for white woman
To jog a path through
And even the wind don't whistle

Even if that space is a place in the middle
Of the jungle with a roof made of palm leaf
And dead nigger skin.

Floors dirt, walls sprawling with green and the natives
All manteled up, still bearing their fangs

WHATEVER WRECKAGE REMAINS

Whatever wreckage remains white flight salvage it. Opportunity is contained
within every bent offering of metal, every heap of soldered skin.
Besides, we are nothing
if not survival; the divine's reclaimed property cached for gold. Everything else
--bury it. Build here on what was: A fraction. A fiction. Menagerie of want.

…because what we want are the things of dreams: A painted red table, doors lockless and open;
A porch off which to spit and sip tea, with a rifle on one arm and in the other an heir.
We want cupboards filled. Our cups running over with karma-full
enough to build anew and relish it—
        the tatted up cities. The factories, their smokestacks. The
        sundowns, rail cars, water fountains, lunch counters…

Let's begin again.

Whatever wreckage remains while flight, salvage it. Opportunity is lost
with the waning light and with the search called off 'til morning, until always
some other morning, when the eyes are fresher and accurate—a count of the ruin, impossible
Claim the shallow things and the things with pulse and the
patchworked gardens and the brass winged things
Hollow out the museums and the mausoleums. Bury our dead
in the delicate labels and in fabricated gold and all
With the same crypted hands that built their cities, tear them down.

ENGLEWOOD, CHICAGO
    -after Lucas Howell's Marble Creek, ID

Google—the God knowable Earth—is sorry
It cannot calculate the distance from Englewood
to Marble Creek. It gives no explanation,

as a god need never do for such inadequacy,
though clearly, it's evidenced their existence.

The one, a windy rocky canyon
steeped in aspen and light
two brothers in a cheap truck trolled
maybe drunken, maybe bored
because the trout wouldn't bite
and because animals outnumber people
ten-to-one

The other, a skillfully crafted sequence of parallel lines
Inside a skillfully crafted sequence
of parallel lines that marks the streets
which are not to be crossed,
because the ops or whatever
and where the animals outnumber people
ten-to-one

In the other is where I sit, alone, behind the wheel
of my exemplar of American innovation,

American salvage idling in the gray morning's
Unplowed streets. My tires and my will almost worn
Having failed to gain traction, failed
To champion us up out this space once saved
By a lawn chair, a mop & bucket, the whole kitchen sink
For somebody who isn't me. I don't care

I can't claim any love for this
Slice of the city's sweetly errant myth—
To claim is not to keep

There is a war on, and we both know soldiers
Who've seen too much, and still, the engine's vibration,
Like my own blood pumping,
For naught.

Maybe a neighbor rouses from the depths
Of his sleep. Pulls on his boots, his hat, his gloves.
Maybe he tells me when to turn the wheel,
When to gas it, when to stop—

The physics of wishing

We put our whole bodies into this propulsion forward
But with no traction, no precision with shifting gears,
no direction, no special tires to tread on water by,
Plus no known Jesus to hook up the hurry up,
it's a wonder we ever make it out these streets alive.

I WANT TO GO HOME
                    -after Warsan Shire

I want to go home again
But home is a box on the block
With an "X" marked
For destruction

The box, now a lot
Where X goes to die—

Last stop
Before the epoch
On the corner of every block
Packs X in a box &
Endeavors for whosoever
Wants to live again
In Christ

I want to go home again
But home is a lock
With the key broke off inside
& I'm in the cross-
Walk, with a map in my hand
And a Glock to my head

X from the same block
Fighting for the same plot
We don't even own

I want to go home
But the clock ticking
The stock dropping
& we ain't ready to buy

X off its axis
Back on the auction block—
turning division into ends &
someone else pockets the change

RARELY BREAK BREAD WE

Rarely break bread we
Anymore a thing
That sits its separate
Lot and speaks when
Only spoken—
The months in
Laugh away prayer
& sinew & sinew & sinew
like skein to needle
its tells to tale--
Every necessary leaving
Every necessary return

In Just Summer

In just summer
bloodlust
the brass band
of ice cream truck
pride all down
the front of my pretty
sunny dress
Mama yellin' mess
& my fresh-pressed hair
carried out of tune
Ice cream man
all down my block
night wearin' thin
in his eyes
The music frizzed
to high heaven
Mama yellin,
boys on the corner
drippin' sun
all up & down
this street

MISSED CONNECTION

Dreadlocked apostle,
I'm so high off you right now.
Not sure if you remember me: I'm the one
That passed you on the street today
Rockin' the grandma sweater in summer,
Two braids in my hair.
You were with your friends, mockin'
The circus folk style. Was like, IDGAF,
And tickled pink that the sky is blue,
To which I replied "pigment is just
A figment of the imagination,"
Though no one was talking to me.
You said something through a mouth
That did not move, your lips
The color of earth
When nothing can grow from it.
And your eyes had their shades pulled down,
So maybe you didn't notice me waving,
A raggedy black flag
Slung around the bus stop pole
On the corner where you work,
Your size elevens grooved into the sidewalk
Your back against the wall,
Holding the whole 'hood down

Box the Girl

box of girl
skin stitched
at the scalp like
a thousand
tiny stars
scarring the sky
carved curve
of her
face lifted
perfectly
to a hand
cracked open
her smile
like a painted
on porcelain
doll eyes
far off & close
when she lies
her arms
all the way open
hair slicked
the air licked stale
the sweet,
sweet man
shook the baby
broke open throw
the whole girl
away

GIRL GONE

It's funny—these women, simply
Walking down the street
Zipping and unzipping the bodies
That hold them in

It must be some sort of game
They play—like Hide-and-Seek—
Into the arms of some lover
Or the sea, only
The places they go to hide
No one can ever find them

Or, no one even looks

It is difficult to remember names
faces, a peculiarity that makes one
woman different from the others—

gapped teeth, tattoos on the ankle
a birthmark at the temple
in the shape of a tree

It is difficult to remember these women
did not just disappear
but were stolen from their lives.

We are told that wherever they are
They want to be

That it was just a fight with a lover
And to give it a few days

And when a few days pass,
We are told nothing at all—a disappearance
Of a whole other kind

We are told to forget

Only a tiny world pauses at the corner
Waiting for these women to climb back in

The larger one ambles on, stalking the streets
Back and forth—the same routes taken

by these women who have grown into air

We cannot blame it for not seeing what is not there

And, when we think about it, what never was

NOTES

Garden Statues takes its title from Al-Siddiq Al-Raddi's poem of the same name, and its inspiration from a photograph by Roy DeCrava, included in 50 Great Black and White Photographs from the Masters of Photography-Part 1 at 121clicks.com

Quoted text in *Corps* comes from President George W. Bush's December 18, 2005 primetime address regarding the Iraq war, as reported by Pete Yost and Terence Hunt in their article "We are winning" for The News-Hearld.

The End and the Beginning is based off of Stanislaw Baranczsk and Clare Cavangh's translation of Wislawa Szymobrska's poem of the same name.

The lines in *Tomorrow's Daily Caller Headline* were taken almost verbatim from the comments section of the satirical Wonkette article "Hero Georgia Cop Ready To Shoot Black Kids Building Treehouse, As Thugs Sometimes Do" http://wonkette.com/545923/hero-georgia-cop-ready-to-shoot-black-kids-building-treehouse-as-thugs-sometimes-do#o0dgXM5wmFM7j5a2.99

Brokedown Palace borrows its name from David Arata's 1999 movie of the same title which borrows its title from the 1970 song by The Grateful Dead

Englewood, Chicago draws its inspiration from Lucas Howell's poem "Marble Creek, Idaho" published in the 2008 Winter/Spring edition of Spoon River Review

I Want to Go Home draws its inspiration from the following lines of "Home" by Warsan Shire

i want to go home,
but home is the mouth of a shark
home is the barrel of the gun

ACKNOWLEDGEMENTS

Thank you to the community of Englewood, which informed and inspired many of these poems. You truly are a gem.

Thank you to Angie Cruz, editor and Arielle Greenberg, guest editor of Asterix Journal, in which Aubade and # first appeared

Thank you to the Columbia College Chicago Poetry Department and my workshop-mates, most especially Annmarie O'Connell, poet and all-around badass, for your continued support and inspiration and Cora Jacobs, photographer, poet and managing editor of Court Green, for fighting for me that one time.

Thank you to my family for your love and support. Special thank you to my husband Ty for your help in the making of this book. I appreciate your patience, love and encouragement (and finally seeing things my way!); to Bernard, who taught me to see bigger and to my mother who's cheered for me the longest and the loudest. When I told you I wanted to go to school to study poetry, you told me to do what I love, and I can't imagine a more encouraging response to such a ridiculous endeavor.

www.ingramcontent.com/pod-product-compliance
Lightning Source LLC
Chambersburg PA
CBHW051409290426
44108CB00015B/2216